Liv Torc is a razor blade [illegible] dian, who plunges the vast [illegible] the human condition, arm[illegible] e of lyrical wonder.

An experienced and po[illegible] hop leader, Liv was the S[illegible] onal Radio 4 Poetry Slam, the second Bard of Exeter and poet in residence at Exeter's first Poetry Festival. She is co-host of The Hip Yak Poetry Shack and runs a successful spoken word stage at WOMAD festival.

Liv works on large-scale poetry and education projects within the South West, including a three-year Paralympic project with Bournemouth University, which culminated in a performance at Westminster in front of parliament. Liv also worked as lead artist on a Somerset wide mental health project called Word/Play. Liv is now a recognised expert on poetry and isolation, working with young people with physical disabilities and adults with mental health challenges.

You can find out all you want to know about her by googling Liv Torc and watching countless clips on YouTube, or visit her website www.livtorc.co.uk

# Show Me Life

Special Edition

Liv Torc

Burning Eye

BurningEyeBooks
Never Knowingly
Mainstream



This edition published by Burning Eye Books 2018
www.burningeye.co.uk

@burningeyebooks

Burning Eye Books
15 West Hill, Portishead, BS20 6LG

ISBN 978 1 90913 6 540

Front cover image adapted from the original taken by Neil Pinnock, as part of the Wildways body painting project.

# Show Me Life

Special Edition

*For Rich, Matilda and Wilfred*

*(and also for me)*

# CONTENTS

# INTRODUCTION

# THIS IS NOT A LOVE POEM

This is not a love poem
it's a note on the fridge
that I didn't bother to write
because we don't have any post-its
or alphabetised fridge magnets
or marker pens.

This is not a hot flush decomposing on paper
and I'm not totally consumed
by an oxytocin monsoon
unable to drag my attention
from the mere mention
of your name
now that at least part of our names
are the same.

This is not an apology
even though I am putting our stuff in a poem again
and I forgot to push the bar stools in last night
and I know how much that annoys you
especially in the dark.

This is not a begging letter
for more dirty, animalistic, eye contact sexcapades
and less flatulence inducing vegetable stews
it's not that personal
or that rude
but is willing to be misconstrued.

This is not a moment of appreciation
for your incredibly well-balanced and sensitive support
for my never ending weight loss endeavours
painful gynaecological furniture extractions
and fickle Gemini superficialities
it's just some words
unwilling to go unheard.

This is not a love poem
so don't you dare get excited
and rush home to read it.
only to feel unintentionally let down
despite the obvious warning in the title.

This is not a desperate note
to tell you that I am secretly plotting my suicide
so if you unexpectedly die
I won't have to waste precious time being alive
knowing you're not.

We have already agreed not to die...
and this is not a piece of dramatic irony
borrowed from a tragic future.

It's a note on the fridge.
with an obvious romantic subtext

reminding you to pick up some soya milk.

# ALL ROADS…

# PER ROMA

Thin crust
Lip lust
Must thrust
Rome
You woke me up
Cake coated finger slut
Slick smoking pavement strut
Cheekbones sharp enough to cut
You slipped your sneak thief fingers
In my brain and stole my rut
Pinched my butt

You caught my breath
Filled my lungs with lust and death
Sieged my heart and my senses
Knocked down my cultural defences
With gender specific plural tenses

Rome
You showed me how to taste delight
Made my clothes a tad too tight
Left me stumbling awestruck through
A crumbling humbling building site
Of holy might and ancient fight

Rome
You found my courage
And my nerve
Every time I crossed a curb
I could dance to every word
No matter if it was spat or slurred

Rome
A sensory pleasure dome
In towering terracotta stone
A pizza paradise of cheesy, sleazy
Eat until you feel uneasy

Sweaty betty, drown in gelati
Mozzarella and spaghetti

Rome
Marble slick limoncello streets
Fir trees full of parakeets
A place where eyes stop
And truly meet

Rome
You woke me up
Turned me on
Lit a spark
I thought was gone.

# PER VENEZIA

I can't coin you,
not in a blink, a click, a word.
You're too big, too grand,
too ephemeral to understand:
every vista is a slight of hand
every window is a Fresco.
You fall apart like a poem in my palm.

You are impossible to define
even harder to explain.
My words get lost and tangled
in your interchanging lanes.
Drown in your blue green liquid veins.

A merry-go-round moving ever faster.
A rabbit warren of little bridges
and apricot hue plaster.
The most beautiful ship wreck lost at sea.
A creaking merchant vessel
clinging to her history.

You have no centre and no heart.
You are an exquisite work of art:
a misty cloud of lonely bards
shuffling your streets and shops
like playing cards.

Of all the mighty man made places
you are the land of masks
with a thousand faces.

# BRIDPORT

Built upon the entrails of the ocean,
dragged from the English Channel in fishing nets
knotted by dexterous Dorset fingers,
the same fingers that wove the hangman's noose.

Mermaid's bones make up the pallor of the pavements
and the ghostly tentacles of giant squid
curl around the grocery stalls
and up the walls of family butchers.

Every publican is a jolly pirate
and antique knickknacks wash up twice weekly
on the market tide,
punk seagulls ride motorbikes up and down the yellow lines
squawking and throwing their chips in the air.

Bridport vibrates with migrate primates,
coffee dates and artist leisure breaks.
It's an underwater Mardi Gras on land
that gets a little frisky but never out of hand.

Salty like the sea bed,
earthy like pasties and pint glasses.
It's a mish mash
of Burbury, Bo-Ho and the waxed moustache,
a place where the broken poor
scratch for food upon the rocky shore
while the finest tweed queue amidst the slimy weeds.

If you listen carefully
you can hear the tinkle of trawler boats bobbing in West Bay
30 miles and one county from the nearest motorway,
built out of rope and fossils,
it will not wash away.

Bridport is a place you go by accident
and then decide to stay.

# IT STARTED WITH…

# THE KISS

When you make a great kiss
it should take you on a journey down the rabbit hole
feet first without a harness
diving into the deepest calmness
but starting with a gentle swim in the warm shallows
soft as falling into a bag of melting marshmallows.

Like laying yourself out naked on a glass table
the right kiss can freeze time, it can disable
twist your lips inside a dunkin' donut sugar bender
extreme kisses mingle rough and tender.
If it is truthful, a kiss can fly
and on occasion make a grown man cry.

Give your kiss willingly
don't pimp it.
Don't chain it up
don't gimp it.
Slip your kiss
whip your kiss into a tango
dip it in mango
make it do the fandango.

A good kiss should accommodate with compassion
that awkward teeth clashing moments
when two ivory broadswords meet in battle
like a brace of shopping trolleys
colliding in the supermarket isle,
the right kiss should slow the pace
force the runners into single file
invite each one to leap like waves
crashing off the surface of a smile.

It should laugh off the unfortunate bubblegum transference
or the gift-wrapped burp
the escaping drool or the tongue-tied slurp
meet head-on the angry chicken pecker

ignore the remnants of the Kit Kat
and the Double Decker.

A true kiss should say goodbye illicitly
speak of back alley duplicity
reach for your genitals but pierce your heart
and smoulder with a fire so passionate
they have to pull your smoking eyelashes apart.

Oh kisses can be stupid, fumbled, desperate, raw
but a great kiss is impossible to ignore
it stays with you, it lays with you
it unsettles your happy home
and for one precious lip locked moment

that kiss will make you feel
a little less
alone.

# YOUR FACE

I have a thing about your face
it is my personal obsession
I like to take pictures of it while you sleep
then post them on Facebook...

Your face has distracted me from worldly affairs
prevented me from pursuing a potential career as an
international diplomat or environmental scientist
Because of your face I have written a lot less poetry
Because of your face I have spent less time looking at my face.
Your face has replaced my interest in the human race
Clouds move across your face with the grace of gently
roaming wildebeests.

If anyone tried to deface, erase or debase your face
with a can of toxic mace
or any other dangerous household substance
I would track them across five continents,
only to break down at their feet weeping
at the deep unfathomable sadness of humanity.

It's a broody, moody, groovy, outwardly attitudey face
It's a slanted face, a never take for granted face
Your face twinkles with freckle sprinkles
and amusing half formed wrinkles
Your cheekbones are like the wings of an eagle
frozen in mid-plummet
Your lips pucker like a ripened strawberry punnet
Stars shine from the wine of your skin
and your nose is like the bow of a perfect violin.

I would like to mass-produce a jelly mould of your face
and sell it to ASDA and to places where there is no ASDA,
only Tesco
putting your great face, inside their shame face,
so that your non-consumerist, anti-capitalist light
can shine out from their shelves
and make them ashamed of themselves.

If I get my way, your raspberry jelly visage
will be covered in blue smarties
at a hundred thousand children's parties.

I want to see your face crocheted in doily lace
and given to every mental case to rest their flower vase.

I want to watch your face grow old...
not cold... not closed down,
set in permanent old man frown
under faded kingly broken crown.

I want to see your face winking at me
from the face of my children
reminding me for eternity
that I will never have it so good
as your face.

I want your face to be my final resting place.
and even after we're both long dead
no longer lying nose to nose in our bed
when we're just a billion atoms
floating in the infinity of space

I want you to know
I'll still have a thing about your face.

# NOT THINKING ABOUT IT

# THE WET PATCH

Lying between us
like a castle moat,
cold and claggy
as drying concrete,
graffitied with our trickling sweat
We have pinned the bed's rosette,
scrawled out the night's vignette
without regret.

A finger deep
puddle swirl,
a penis hurl
through black coarse curls,
a molten pearl
shot through a girl.

A damp wet slap against the skin
that comes from somewhere
deep within,
a thigh surprise,
a leg baptise,
a sticky slippery
glidey slide
to lay beside.

The highest tide
of the sex ride.

This is life being lived
and this is non-life
never happened.
This is lust glue,
the coo-coo-ca-choo
of genital kung fu,
this is my joy in you
dancing with your inner goo.

This is the spunk of pure potential,
a slingshot of something existential
made inconsequential
by our giggles.

Now seeping outwards
across a lake
of silent cotton,
soaking downwards
into secret mattress drains,
what could have been
a billion human remains
end up as unexplained stains.

We give it little thought
as we roll back then reattach,
you the perfect gentlemen
prove that you're the perfect catch,
as you lay your body like a coat

across the lovely patch.

# I (LOVE) UD

Such a funny little thing:
Bakelite with ratted wire hair
a sperm snare,
the cave's angry copper bear
lurking somewhere underneath the underwear.

My past protector
an interesting mathematical vector
an egg and womb disconnector.

A catholic symbol of disgrace
the minimiser of the human race,
the relief upon my morning after face.

You're a physical pincher,
a grab the hot water bottle wincer.
The tickler of todgers.
The antenna of rogers.
The Christmas fairy on the cervix tree.
The bouncer at the door to Club Fertility.
You're Mr T,
adorned in all his metallic finery.

You're a piece of vagina fascinator fashion
that must be fitted with compassion.
with high strung sins
and low strung strings,
you flex your wire womb wings,
beat back the sci-fi changelings
and therefore save entire communities
from invasion by strange albino children
with Machiavellian mind control powers
and 1970s roll neck jumpers.

Yes you're the result of war torn feminist striving,
60s contraception and sexual arriving.
You are the seed of liberation and revolution.

The key to China's one child solution.
The pin in the side of evolution.

You're not about death
you're all about sieving,
deciding when to keep out
and when to let in the living.
You're not about failing to rejoice
in procreation's primal voice.
You're all about choice.

Such an iconoclastic piece of plastic
with a purpose so fantastic.
You give permission for the morning glory.
You put the T
in the female story,
so we're not sory.

You have made sex free
or at least as free as it can be
in all its sensual heart breaking brutality.
You have given so much depth to me,
prepared me better for maturity, maternity...

So now as I ponder pollination
with thoughtful reticence and flirtation,
I open my legs once more in celebration
of the most powerful letter in uncreation.

# THINKING ABOUT IT

# MAYBE IT'S...

Maybe it's complicated
or maybe it's really fucking simple.
Maybe this is what always happens in the end
or in the middle, or before a big catastrophic change.

Maybe I need to break a leg,
I mean for real, not just metaphorically
or maybe I need to break a heart,
a broken heart could be the only way to ignite the spark.

Maybe I need a bad one-night stand
in the back of a lorry on the M27
with a anarchistic performance artist in tie-dye dungarees.
Maybe I need a couple more post-modernist degrees.

Maybe I got old, or at least older
and I've spunked out all the spunk
that used to keep me spunky.
Maybe I got happy.

Maybe I have shouted out all my anger
and have no anger left to shout.
Maybe I've run out of saliva.

Maybe, like smoking, rage and self-righteous indignation
only look cool when tripping off the tongue
of someone very young, still under 31,
maybe I have lost 'The Fun'.

Maybe I've closed down,
gone inwards, built too many walls.
Maybe I don't like people anymore.
Maybe it's my thirties.
Maybe it's my marriage.

Maybe I got too big, went too far.
Maybe I'm not going any further.
Maybe I'm too fat, or too full.
Maybe I'm not sexy anymore,

not as sexual as before.

Maybe I don't need the applause
like I used to need the applause.
Maybe I'm not lonely anymore.

Maybe I've collected all my books
and train tickets and dreams
put them in that boat
and floated them down the river
with my name,
and I'm just standing on the bank watching them go
and feeling nothing.

Maybe I no longer feel the shiver of the universe upon my skin
or maybe I am the universe and the shiver
and the current of the river.
Maybe I've found peace.

Maybe that uncharted hole of emptiness
that I have carried around all my life
has gone.
Maybe I am free.
Maybe I want a new adventure.
Maybe I want a baby.

Maybe the road less travelled by
leads to a really nice picnic spot
and infinity is not only in a grain of sand
but also in my own pupils.

Maybe it's complicated
or maybe it's really fucking simple.

Maybe I don't have anything left to say.

# LET'S HAVE A BABY?

Should we have a baby?
Yes, let's have a baby
Although I'm really too lazy
to deal with a baby.

Oh let's have a baby
Let's make one right now
We've been practising for ages
I think we know how.

Oh let's have a baby
I'm broody and heated
But my energy's precious
I don't want it depleted.

Oh let's not have a baby
Babies are weird
The pressure the smell
are things to be feared
Plus you'll end up with vomit
woven into your beard.

Let's not have a baby
There are too many babies
that grow into people
who then grow into cars
Let's wait until after
they colonise Mars.

But our baby might change things
be king of the school
Fight social injustice
make the planet more cool.

Oh let's have a baby
Babies are life
A baby would make me
a much better person and wife.

Let's not have a baby
I want to keep my career
and the thought of nine months
without wine gin or beer.

Besides our house is a danger
full of sockets and edges
and I don't want to mush things
or purify veggies.

Oh let's have a baby
Or perhaps even two
It's what every couple
in their thirties should do.

Oh let's have a baby
You could wear a papoose
I'd do kegal crunches
to make my vagina less loose.

Let's not have a baby
It would ruin our love
A baby is like a penile chastity glove
*It's better not to dwell too much*
*On the sentence above.*

This is a really big question
Let's take time to think
Sit down on the sofa
with a very large drink.

Let's not have a baby
We really aren't sure
Plus a baby is harder
than a plant to ignore.

Oh let's have a baby
It would fill both our hearts

and give me a reason
for these lady parts.

Let's have a baby
I want to pass on our genes
nurture potential
and support fledgling dreams.

Oh let's have a baby
to live on in our stead
Someone to walk in our shoes
once we're dead.

Or is it just selfish
to want a child in your wake?
Would having a baby
be a stupid mistake?

Oh look at that baby
all peaceful and dreaming
Then ten seconds later
Shitting and screaming.

Oh let's not have a baby
Let's not have a baby
Oh let's have a baby, a baby, a baby
I think I am starting to go a bit crazy.

So let's not have a baby
Opt for natural selection
Refuse to add another pawn
to the human collection.

No I'm sure it won't matter
If we don't use protection.

# BEING

You are on stage right now, with me
your potential is inside me
buried in the folds of something primal,
flesh or cell or memory.

You with your existence in the balance
between choice and circumstance,
your destiny pacing round
the holding pen of souls
ready to unroll like a carpet
across space and time
waiting for a big bang.

We have started talking you and I
in the car, on the sofa, late at night,
you who may never be anything more
than a nudge, a thought, a fear
implanting images in my brain
with all your powers of persuasion,
us in the bath, covered in crumbling bubbles,
hand in hand
bimbling down dusty roads
with colourful rucksacks
sandwiches, butterflies
and sacrifice.

You, who I have not invited,
who I didn't think I wanted,
have started to extract from me
a love so sickeningly epic
it feels like magnetic plates searing vast valleys
in the continents of who I thought I was.

I am not an easy customer,
so determinedly rational,
so busy with all my beautiful hobbies,
other more glamorous dreams.

but I hear you calling
from the bottom of a forgotten wishing well,
I hear the purple music that you're making
with those tiny conductor batons
that you stole from ribs and flotsam.

A billion years
of instinct and evolution
plucking at my strings.

# THE QUICKENING

# MORNING SICKNESS

I've come to the conclusion
that it's a right of passage;
a vomitus assault on dry land,
a grumpy hangdog of green bilious fumes
corroding normal life.
The only thing steady in this tsunami
of shifting inner ooze
is the sofa.
The only thing certain is flatulence.

I find myself empathising with crotchety,
door slamming, stick waving,
old men in council flats.
There is no question that I am becoming someone else,
an uncomfortable angry person
with a malevolent distrust of shrimp.
Regarding offers of food like a cat might regard
a man in a clown outfit.

I want to hide in the hydrangea bushes
wearing beige flannel pyjamas
eat mash potato and fish fingers
at 3 o'clock in the morning
with cutlery carved from frozen lemonade.

I don't want to go into the kitchen
I don't want to empty the bins
and I certainly don't want to open the fridge
to smell the cheese.

Star jumps are over for me.
So is rhyming poetry.
No mega enzyme wheatgrass.
No scrolling.
No reversing.
No sense of humour.
There is only the security of wotsits
and I'm not even sure about those now.

I am a grey ungrateful exhausted air bag
unable to see the beauty
in the symptoms of new life.
A pallid sunken Gollum
in acupressure wristbands.

I would do almost anything to give this feeling away,
just for the afternoon,
preferably to my husband.

# SHOW ME LIFE

Take me to the little room
With the sonic zoom
Smear jelly on my belly
Put a picture on the telly
Show me life
Sick-making
Hip-shaking
Breath-taking life.

# BABY VEGETABLE FRUIT THING

Poppy seed poppet
Sesame mess in me
Elemental lentil
Kidney bean kid
Cum consequential kumquat
Late date primate
Limey alien inner ugh squish
Little Poddington Pea
Lemon tree
Apple of my inner thigh
Large tomato small potato
Banana karma internal drama
Flutter nut butter squash
Baby vegetable fruit thing
Frantically trying on salad slippers
Until you become a pumpkin

# BUMPED

# I'M NOT 15

I'm not 15,
I'm not going to snap back
from this skin stretching torture rack,
I'm not going to pop you out like a ping-pong ball
without due carnage to my pelvic floor.
I'm not 15,
I'm 34,
and I'm built more like an apple
than an apple core.

I'm not 15,
I'm scared but I'm not alone
sitting bulbous at a bus stop
texting my baby daddy
on my jewel encrusted mobile phone
ignoring the gentle prodding
in the tiny triangle of my pelvic bone
afraid to go home.

I'm not 15,
I'm not a shy victim
or a school yard slut.
My breasts flail about
they don't point up.
I'm not 15,
with a can of cider and an undercut,
my bits have grown down
as my dreams have grown up.

I'm not 15,
I've lived it through,
done the things that 15, 21, 27, 33 year-olds should do.
I've been defeated,
I've been renamed,
I've been reborn,
I've danced naked in the moonlight
to a leather clad man blowing a Viking horn.

I'm not 15,
I've licked eyes dilated, groins inflated,
healed broken hearts that were self created,
I've had a four-night wild forest solo slumber,
I've shat on a lost love's new phone number.

I've been black dog lonely,
lost friends I can't regain,
painted chemical highs across my brain.
I've faced my faults and my shame,
had a thousand people chant my name,
I'm not the same.

I'm not 15,
I don't have to conform
inside a culturally enforced uniform.
I've earned my woman and my voice,
I can look at my stretch-marks and rejoice.
I don't get excited by fags and celebrity,
I get excited by choice.

I'm not 15,
I'm not going to snap back
from this skin stretching torture rack,
I'm not going to pop you out like a Ping-Pong ball
without due carnage to my pelvic floor.

I'm not 15,
I'm 34,
I look like a woman
with an underscore
and I'm built more like an apple
than an apple core.

# ACCEPTANCE

A day after our silent fight
the bed felt soft and easy
subdued by the storm
warm and a little reborn.

In relief of this cool peace
I moved my heavy hips
so you could curl against me,
as I curled around our unborn child
and let you hold us both.

Only a few hours before
in the aftermath of war
she had revealed herself to us
begrudging, stubborn, camera shy
all hands and feet and life unfurling
hidden inside these two bodies
curling.

Now lying in the sweet hot tonic
of your skin
I held my breath
as for the first time
your arms reached round
to embrace my swelling belly.

# CHANGE ME

I wanted you to change me
So I chose you
Sucked you into me
Fused my bones and muscles
to your bed
Waited.

Cradled you in big pants from M&S
Steamed you in hot baths
with lavender and lemongrass
Rubbed you protectively
in front of strangers
Wore you like a shield
in the sun.

But in the tiny bladder hours
With aching hips
and nightmares
I would lie awake full of you
and thoughtless.

Paddling hard against the tide
of breath blood milk
Padding heavily round the kitchen
in the moonlight
For the first time
I wished myself a man.

My great love
I wait for you
unable to let go
of me.

# NOTES FROM A SMALL ISLAND

*38 weeks pregnant and counting*

I was never really that small before
but now I'm impossible to ignore:
a space hopper slash dinosaur
waddling across the supermarket floor,
low riding an 8lb bowling ball.

Yes I'm Queen of the Oompa Loompas,
Violet Beauregard in hues of blush and sepia,
not so whiny but slightly weepier.
More than just an angry bird on a mission,
I'm a cataclysmically ferocious pufferfish,
catapult me down Frome or Totnes high street
and watch me take out small independent vintage shops
with my flailing arms and explosive posterior depth charges.

Yes, on the outside I'm taking up more and more of the room
but the territory surrounding my lungs, liver and womb
is like a slowly deflating and constrictive balloon.
You're elbowing me out of my strength and my power,
I have to psyche myself up to climb over the bath
and into the shower.

I can't sleep on my front, my back, or my right side,
my dreams are like a surreal Pink Floyd anxiety ride.
I have really clear skin
and plush shiny hair,
but I don't dare to sneeze
in my good underwear.

I can't tie my laces,
or bend down to pick up my shoes,
I can't shave my legs
or even look at my pubes.
I have to buy Double G parachutes
to constrain my dampening boobs.

My bathroom bin is full
of empty Anusol tubes.

Yes it's really quite lovely
to sacrifice and to share
but inside of my belly
it's internal organ warfare
as I sit in a fortress of cushions
gasping half lungfuls of air
and sift through NHS handouts
and gifts of pastel knitwear.

I am itchy and stretching,
drooling and retching,
never less sexy but never more letching
my bladder is full of a raging monsoon
but there's rarely more pee than a tiny teaspoon.
My hips are all achy and my chest feels like lead.
I can't get close to my husband
just hug with my head
and the minute I'm comfy I have to get out of the bed.

Each evening I bleed from my nose, anus and gums,
I binge nightly on Gaviscon and daily on Tums.
I am one body, four eyelids, two heads and four thumbs;
two heart beats, two vaginas and also two bums.

As fat as a pumpkin
with her own inner candle.
It's amazing when determined
what your body can handle;
coaxing and encouraging my significant girth
through the final few days
approaching the moment of birth
when my courage will be weighed
along with my baby and worth.

And I want to say truly that I really don't care

that I'll probably scream,
pooh myself and perennially tear
because all that will matter is you're finally there
out in the open, alive and aware.

That I made you inside me,
from sperm and some cells
and several degrees of indignity hell,

and as long as we get through
with the stamp,
*Mother and baby are well*

that's all I'll remember
and maybe the only story I'll tell.

# BIRTH

# RED BIRD

*On the birth of my first child - with the epidural.*

She is the soft floppy rosy flaky thing we made
that spurted out of me on a Klimt orgasm
of blood and Pethidine
appearing at the end of a magnolia corridor.

A tiny red bird
curled between my calves,
shivering on cool white sheets

mouth gasping, rooting worms
finding only air.

As she arrived through me
like a boat in a bottle neck
I remember thinking,
this is it,
the messy, rippy, screamy, stretchy bit...
the end of it
and it was quick
the biggest shit
and she was crown, head,
shoulders free,
red raw and quivering between my knees
all my remaining energy
pushed into the emergence
of this entity.

The painful echoing reality
dulled by drugs
and lost to memory.

On my breast
she is all eyes and softness,
a sci-fi cone head
covered in dark fine moss,
crowned with a cervix kiss.

My new reality
snuffling inside badly fitting skin,
blue stewed hands

finger nails as small
as the ridges on the outside
of a tax disc.

# THANK YOU

for washing my hair
in the grey grot of the hospital bathroom
and for taping electrodes to my back
as I shook on all fours
with my huge belly
hanging over sagging red pyjamas.
Thank you, for untangling the wires
when they got stuck
in the buttons of my cardigan.

for playing Who Wants To Be A Millionaire
on your iPad
to distract me from the contractions
which, by the way, were the only reason
I kept losing the big money questions,
and after four days
when I couldn't stop crying,
thank you for climbing into my tiny single bed
and breathing my breath.

Thank you for sitting for hours in torturous chairs
and for driving to the hospital
three times in one night
at nearly 100 miles an hour down the A36.
for missing a week of work
even though you had a really important concert
and we needed the money.

Thank you for stroking my feet very lightly
as the epidural touched my spine.
and for helping to clean up all the blood
and shredded bits of me,
despite the fact that you're really squeamish
and hate that sort of thing.

Thank you for actually looking at the head crowning
I never thought you would
and I never thought I'd want you too.

Thank you for holding our daughter
skin to skin.
inside your favourite blue shirt
and for crying on the phone to your mum
as you fed me with smash from a fork.

Thank you for realising
that I'm made of stronger stuff
than you previously suspected.

and thank you
for proving that to me too.

# THE CROWNING

*On the birth of my second child - without the epidural.*

It feels almost impossible to describe
eye popping, scream starting
heart stopping
like your vagina has just entered
the world paper folding championships
and your labia is attempting a flamingo.

So uniquely unexpected
so alien and odd
a canon ball emerging
from a nitrate fog
the blazing morning sun
bursting through sultry sodden clouds
if the sun were a giant pine cone
and the clouds were soft battered cod.

Oh my fucking
Oh my fucking
OH MY FUCKING GOD!!!

A freight train with fingernails
a pineapple on greasy rails
a tsunami with the force to shatter
the *Three Gorges Damn*
a pearl shucked with a spoon
from a reluctant looking clam.

It's not impossible
or terrifying
or even something to be feared
It's just very very
Very very
Very VERY
WEIRD

A seam splitting
Blood spitting
Vadge shitting
Miracle.

And you can't stop it
although you sort of wish you could
as steam starts to billow
from underneath your hood
And you're just staring grimly at a towel rail
and a beige watercolour of some flowers
while in-between your legs
Fred Dibnah is imploding
your industrial flesh towers.

We're talking Big Bang
Pringles pop
in your pants
that you can't stop.

Or at least some minor galaxy emerging
in the place where your pants should be
if they weren't squatting mute and dejected
under a hospital chair with your fear
and that ridiculously ostentatious hospital bag
complete with ginormous sanitary towels
*shaped like Viking death canoes*
and four shelves of *Boots* stocking fillers:
water spritzers, lip balm,
lavender massage oil and slipper socks.

I mean what's the point of a battery operated hand fan
and a packet of glucose sweets
when you are clinging onto the mountain face of life?
While some unknown force throws
giant mirror balls at your pelvis
and a hurricane tears teeth marks in your fibroids.

That's why you have to get so fat,
so you're not blown away by the force of it.
That's why you have to be so fierce
so you can bare your teeth into the wind

and PUSH...

And if I'm honest
it does involve some minor chaffing
more than stubbing your toe on the sideboard
or cricking your neck on the golf course.
After all it's a tiny hole,
a large spherical object
and a colossal force...

So you better live it
and forgive it
and do your best to just breathe with it...
because it's going to take you to the edge
of everything you know.

As your walls melt hot mango
into a gas tinged echo fade
Your eyes dip like breadsticks
into Nescafé and disinfectant flavour shade
Your pelvic floor unhinges
and detonates its mortar
Pneumatic thighs start shaking
in tepid tiger water
calling into being your scrunched up
screaming son or daughter...

And all the while
from the sidelines
Wonder Woman, Princess Leia,
The Lady Galadriel, Artemis, Haumea, Frigg,
Buffy the Vampire Slayer

and your Grandmother's, Grandmother's, Grandmother
are smoking cigars
and chanting your secret power name
As they call up your inner Sheerah
to squash the panic in your brain
Sticking two thighs up like fingers
to Centuries of biblical misogynistic shame.

And it's kind of tragic that evolution
tries to take away the memory of that pain
You earned that jagged piece of stitching
your scars are hissing at the seams.

This is the moment you made life
not some fuzzy hormone altered dream.

It's called the crowning for a reason
it's when you become
A QUEEN.

AFTER BIRTH

# NOT THE SAME WOMAN

I'm not the same woman inside
my womb was a fist
now it's a lopsided smile,
it bends like a bottom lip
quivering.

My skin used to flow
now it charges.

I am no longer a secret.
I am conquered,
a flag in a pile of crumbs
and vomit.

My vanity is a broken mirror
in a bucket.

My vagina is no longer a cunt,
it's a pussy,
shy and afraid
shallow and shell-shocked.

When I reach my fingers between my legs
I am like a teenage boy at a prom
teetering on the edge
of an unknown universe.

# VAGINA POO - A HAIKU

Chip shop curry sauce
Oozing down your sausage legs
Smeared across your happy fanny

# BOOB EYES AND LULLABIES

You are a tiny kangaroo
mouse monkey
with satin finished moleskin spine.
Deep pools of slate grey universe
peek out through your hairless brow.
You are ancient and unblinking
full of primal wonder thinking.

Foetally foldable,
bodily mouldable,
snuffler, grunter,
sweet milky truffle hunter,
squeaker, snorter,
prodigal daughter.
You make my body wobble
as you latch and suck and gobble.
You make me spout insipid twaddle,
my bulimic onesie super model.

You are all flaky fingers,
gaping lips,
fast-peddling
wriggle hips,
boob eyes and lullabies,
piercing air-raid hunger cries,
the Queen of unrest,
nipple obsessed,
rooting and tooting
upon my exploding mountainous
custard dribbling chest.

A deal changer.
A life rearranger.
A familiar stranger
who I must protect from all danger.
A motherly maker.
A social icebreaker.
An every three hours

guaranteed waker.
You are an everything giver
and an everything taker.

Staring down my droopy
sleep deprived eyes,
inexplicably wise
with fascination and need
like I am your whole future and life
the thing we're both living for,

then looking right through me
as if I'm not there at all.

# TITS IN THE PITS

I'm not really into my boobs.
Can I say that?
As a feminist, as a mother,
as a nipple sensitive tongue twisting
'what the hell' kind of lover.

Can I slap them out like black jacks and fold,
flop out my bad hand of fleshy no man's mammary land,
give it up as a bad gland or two?
Is that ok with the beauty paradox?
Is that ok with you?

To be both accepting
and yet not
of all the wobbly bits I've got,
but still like myself a lot?

To love the milk
but wave flaming torches at the cow?
To want less junk in my top trunk
less brunt to my front?
Something quieter,
something smaller
that doesn't require GPS
and a high altitude explorer.

In the very least make them equally divided
so they don't appear lopsided
especially in H&M four-way changing mirrors
which instead of making women
over the age of 25
feel like badly put together potatoes
should have been alarming the world
to the 'leggings are not trousers' disaster of recent years.

No I'm not really into my boobs.
They are not my 'girls'.

They are my alcoholic aunties
rolling around in porridge,
my bad pennies that never turn up,
a juggler grappling pumpkins under a handkerchief.

Big boobs are the pits
they live in the pits, literally.

But where I feel shame
(and a slight curvature of the vertebrae)
she sees only life:
they are the salivating, gasping,
desperate gulping air of the drowning,
the only brains left in a world full of zombies
and she found them first.

They are the jubbly jellies of all-nighter cuddles
in front of flickering tellies,
the soda-streams of baby dreams.

Accessible, free, beloved and handy,
they are Calpol and Nightol and Dettol and brandy.

Her baby lust for my bust
makes me feel like a topless Scarlet Johansson
in a locker room full of 17 year old rugby players.
In her half closed, rolled back, perfect-day eyes,
in her happy suckling whimper cries,
the whole time, space, quantum physics of it,

the whole perky, pixelated,
insidious undermining of female awesomeness
by continuous comparisons to swimsuit model potential... of it
just flows
away
on a current of milk
and primal monkey power

and we are beautiful,
all four of us,
at least when we don't have to think about it.

And if my baby girl
were to grow up and grow out,
with a similar clout,
if her knockers were shockers,
a couple of dockers,
I ardently wish for her no such raging self-doubt
but the pride and the
'not give a fuckness'
to walk with chest brazen and out,
to be selective and potent
but still point them about.
To wear her boobs
like the flags of her country
waving from the mast of her spine.

To love them as much
as she so clearly loves mine.

# NAPPY CHANGING SONG

I love your eyes
I love you chunky little thighs
I love you

I love your nose
I love your toes
I love your woolly little clothes
I love you

I love your ears
I'd love your tears
but your ducts are oddly dry
there is no water when you cry
and I've often wondered why

So I'm just going to put you back in your cot
and have a quick Google.

# BABY-PROOFING THE WORLD

Everything is scarier now
because of her.
The world is bigger and angrier
with sharper teeth
it lurks and jumps and waves
its rusty scissor fingers.
Every town is an upturned draw
full of slippery silver knives
every curb a gaping stair gate.

Unpredictable people in NHS glasses
are no longer quirky and charming
they are knee high glass coffee tables;
I want to cut up tennis balls
and stick them to their elbows.
I want to hermetically seal
toothless cider quaffing wurzels
in their smoky blue halos,
shoot them down over incinerators.
I want to dust off the fireguard
and put it over the sun,
bubble wrap the car and the tarmac
and drive with nursery rhymes blaring
from reinforced windows.

I want to gather together
all the edges, sharp tongues,
bruised clouds, squashed dreams
and poisonous thoughts
put them high up
in the top cupboard
behind the casserole dishes
next to the custard powder.

I want to lock up my marriage
in a safety deposit box,
pack the gaps with polystyrene wotsits

so I can't touch it
or drop it,
or fuck it up
because it is the steel chassis
of the hurtling vehicle
she will drive through the universe.

I want to throw myself bodily
between her and all danger,
the shadowy figure,
the truck,
the tsunami,
the end of the world.
Wrap my arms around her
and sit in the middle of the bed
surrounded by cushions
and friendly looking teddy bears
and never leave the house again.

Because I was huge and brave
and powerful
and now I am small and soft,
my voice is a rattle,
my hands full of butter.

Yes everything is scarier now
because of her...

For we are only as brave
as the faltering smile
of our tiniest child.

THE TERRIBLES

# IF YOU SLEEP THROUGH THE NIGHT

I know you're only three
but if you sleep through the night tonight
I'll give you a whole pot of multi-coloured glitter,
two minutes with the sudocrem without the lid on,
ten pink smarties and three stories about a squirrel.

If you sleep through the night tonight
I'll give you my only pair of glasses to play with
all the teaspoons from the broken drawer in the kitchen
I'll let you press *all* the buttons
on the central heating remote control panel
and I'll let you wear your *Peppa Pig* wellies in bed.

If you sleep through the night tonight
I will make you a golden tinsel belt
and attach your toothbrush to it like a sword
or wand or magical unicorn horn
I'll put five satsumas and six green grapes in the blender
and let you drink them out of our only surviving crystal egg cup

If you sleep through the night tonight
you can have my car keys to play with
and my car, my kidney, my spleen, my tonsils, my other kidney
my iPhone and all my remaining teeth.

If you sleep through the night tonight
I'll pay your *Netflix* subscription for life
and all your university fees,
or bail, whichever, I won't judge you
I won't even look at you funny
over the top of my toddler mangled spectacles.

If you sleep through the night tonight
I will give you the memory
of your Great Grandmother's budgie,
That December in Venice
and that time I spoke to Mick Jagger on the telephone.

If you sleep through the night tonight
I will always sponsor your 'Children In Need'
fancy dress fun runs.

If you sleep through the night tonight
I will chase you through the house
wearing the empty stickle-brick tub on my head
Whispering loudly *I'm going to get you!*
Before falling to my knees
To kiss everyone of your ten tiny toes.

If you sleep through the night tonight...

If you sleep through the night tonight...

If you sleep through the night tonight...

IfYOU SLEEP THROUGH THE NIGHT TONIGHT

Oh bollocks your brother's just woken up.

# FAMILY BED

Moon doily
Snot sponge
Bum scratcher
Crumb clinger
Full body tantrum flinger
Softly softly tuneless singer
Humdinger.

This bed is a protest in defiance of sleep,
it paddles the shallows when you long to plunge deep.

This bed is a jungle with creepers and croaks,
it billows and belches and emits tornados of smoke
This bed is a rickety raft on a rag rugged river,
forging upstream to the milk splattered sea
This bed is a life form
we will one day set free.

This bed is a cave where wolves creep,
curl up in packs of panting paws to sleep
This bed is a den nestled deep in the earth,
it's full of insects and mud and the soft blood of birth.

It has elbows and knee caps,
fuzz swirls of hair,
it has wet wipes and snot stains
and toys it wont share.

This bed is uncuttable,
in a room they can't tax
It's all coughing and cuddles and noses nestled in backs
This bed is a lighthouse when the dark rages outside
and tiny feet patter from nightmares
to snuggle safe at our side.

This bed is a hand brake turn
On a budget magic carpet ride

It is cosy and crowded
and shallow and deep
It is desperately tired
but a long way from sleep.

This bed is restrictive and hard to stretch out,
it has whinging and shhhhing,
and flailing about
It has toddlers and babies
and breasts leaking life,
It has a man hanging helpless,
not touching his wife.

Our bed was for lovers
Full of sweet sweaty sighs
Stickiness slick on staccato thighs
This bed is for parents
with no chance of parole
It has plundered our faces
and swallowed us whole.

Poured us like batter into a pan
One crispy fried woman
One burnt brittle man.

This bed is our children
It's us and it's them
hanging on in there
and counting to ten.

This bed is a journey
we are too tired to make,
Our eyes deliberately closed
even though we're always awake.

This bed is a blip in a life full of lazing
This bed is disgusting
This bed is AMAZING.

A moment
Some seconds
A fistful of time
A memory so liquid
it will spill down the years.

To be served up with tea
and my old lady tears.

It's my howl
My heart break
My Wolf Mother's shout
But right now it's cold
and it's mingin'

So I'm going to GET OUT!

# LIMITS

It's very difficult
Loving this much,
against so much resistance.

So I doubt myself
I question whether I can actually do it
Whether my body can hold itself together long enough
to see them hold themselves together.

My hair has dreaded at the back
My eyes wobble
My hands are cracked from all the liquid
they have sucked from me
I wonder if my sacrum will unhinge
my hips fall off
and one day while carrying them both up the stairs
I will suddenly without warning
collapse like badly constructed Lego.

So I find myself shouting
and hating myself for shouting
ashamed that I am the sort of parent
the sort of person, who shouts
And in that moment I realise
that my edges
my limits
are here.

Not in the exam hall or dance floor
Not in the incident room,
with a backlit map and ringing telephones
Not at the side of the road staring at twisted metal
or starving on a mountain.

But here
on the front room carpet
as I catch my two-year-old
riding her baby brother like a show pony.

# KNOCK THE KNOCKERS ON THE HEAD

I'm really very sorry poppet
but I am a cliff face with no crags
A fading MILF with two joyless chewed up hessian bags
You can scramble, chew and scream
but I have no handle for your latch
I am your mummy have no doubt
but I'm not the ever-ready heartbeat steady
hot, close, oozing, life-force sauce
for your toddler fish and chips

I'm not your mummy bitch.

I know I have the walnuts
and you're all about the walnut whips
but there comes a point when every mother
has to plant a flag
in her own tits.

# YES TERRIBLE

Nothing has ever challenged
my sense of self and humanity
like a two year old
in full fist chewing,
body convulsing,
brake screaming glory.

Like a tiny prison riot in a nappy,
Scarlet O'Hara on a tequila meltdown,
the eye of Irma in a shot glass.

It's physically restraining,
happiness draining
wee, tears, snot, blood or shit staining
lion taming.
advanced combat defence training.

You literally get head butted in the face
and have to apologise
for spitting up blood
and making a scary yelping noise.

The trigger can be no bigger
than a broken plastic figure
a sibling tussle, a snarky bicker
the curling edges of a sticker
a drippy Mr. Whippy
the escapologist balloon
the preferred size, shape and colour
of a morning yogurt spoon.

The location has no bearing
except on the number of people who are staring
it also helps if what you're wearing
rides up, falls down or gapes apart
as you press the convulsing little body
to the ping pong panic of your heart.

Weddings, funerals, the M26
in immediate proximity to fire pits,
rusty nails, extreme gales
perilously corroded handrails
ice cream van exhaust trails
on the bodies of sleeping snails.

When you are having a poo
especially when you are having a poo.

But specifically in the vicinity of landscaped privet hedges
in the shape of ornamental fruit
in front of a man in his 50's wearing beige trousers
and reading the *Sunday Telegraph*,
who serves you his eyebrows like a custody summons
as you limp apologetically towards the exit,
small child boarded under your armpit
like a souvenir from the shrieking shack.

And despite your best attempts
to reach the car before you start crying
you find yourself curled up on cold lino
arms wrapped like Broadmoor bed bondage
around the stuttering, quacking, violently shaking
molten core of a space rocket
trying to launch itself at the sun
through the keyring carousel
in a National Trust gift shop.

Yes

They are terrible

So very terrible

A kalashnikov kaleidoscope
A *Cath Kidston* King Kong

All impulse
no control
A late night Trump tweet
An air freshener that smells faintly of Napalm
and the 2017 USA/North Korea
nuclear disarmament negotiations.

No nothing unravels the gravel
of my personal driveway to sanity
more than a two year old
experimenting with their emotions

*Except maybe a President.*

Like a painter trying to depict
a country scene of an amiable cow
and a twinkly eyed peasant woman
using only a bucket of red gloss paint
and a welding torch.

They are demented
They are why gin was invented
They are future Christmas anecdotes
full of fist-chewing and near misses

Only EVER two seconds away
from being swept off the pavement
and covered liberally in kisses.

And three seconds away
from being dragged out of a shop by their feet
and left face up in a puddle
in-front of a Noddy sit and ride.

# GRIT OVER TIME

# HAIRLOOM

You take three equal strands,
one of time,
one of grit,
one of blood.

Thick as adders
sheer as the finest pantyhose
the brambliest bouffant
Section sharply
plait deftly.

Blood over grit
Time over blood
Grit over time.

We've passed on this miracle of molecular curls
From grandmother's fingers
To great granddaughter's twirls
This head thatch,
Heron's nest
Top down winter vest
Thermal fitted backrest.

My chest fringe,
Candle singed
Upside down Medusa minge.

My wind machine's war cry
A merkin manufacturer's bulk buy
Five packets of L'Oréal for every
*I'm not worth the salon*
home hair dye.

A chaetophobes Chernobyl
A trichophilia tease
A tidal wave of tussled tassels
A horror hive for imprisoned bees.

It grows in bushels and lava trails,
Swallows space
Snags zips
A total scalp eclipse
Quick sand for curvy grips
Catapulting clamps, claws and crocodile clips
Demanding gymnastics from its elastics
It's so big,
it's almost sarcastic.

Flowing like hay from a gerbil tray
down the matriarchal line
18 amino acids on an inter-generational paradigm.

Blood over grit
Time over blood
Grit over time.

Grandma Pamela clings onto her last few silver strands
Feet precariously dangling above the universe
Swollen eyes staring through beige bed bars
*She's got the Barwood hair*, she beams
Sucking green goo from a brown beaker
Touches her cloud quaffed candy floss with shaking fingers
Once a rope of flaxen wool
turned to spider dust.

My daughter, her great granddaughter
like her, like me, will forever be
the scourge of snippers and plungers.

When my mum was a girl
Pamela made her sleep every night
in drum tight plait tails
Taking one out in turn to smooth and rebind.
Never allowing both to know freedom or each other
Imprisoned in a permanent parting.

Now I sit every morning
with glitter bands and paddle brush
Tease out the tangles,
as she squirms and screams
My hands, Pamela's hands, their hands
The women who stand in the marrow of my bones
with their grit and their combs.

My *Cousin It* impression
Was their *Cousin It* impression
and would have been hers and hers and hers
Instead my fore-bearers were boofing it up
like Marie Antoinette, Beethoven, Einstein, Samson
Weaving it into blankets
to wrap around their follically flamboyant offspring
so they could live on
to carry the steel strands of our essence
down the generations to this moment.

Where the HAIR LOOM
hangs on in there
Flying about my face
like fifty contemporary dances
trying to prove the boundaryless potential of space.

This rare conflagration of DNA and dandruff
The literal chain that binds my grandmother
to my daughter, my mother to me
reaching down through the strands of destiny.

A legacy shoot
Rapunzel's last escape route
A cosmic relay race
That not only ensures our survival
but really frames the face.

Passed down from hair to heir and heir to hair

Towards an unknown future
where it will be used to tie the continents back together,
synthesize bird skeletons,
or strangle a mutant giraffe.

........

The girl with the Kim Kardashian eyebrows
and magpie blue highlights
blow dries the chain, the helix, the family snare
In pouty despair
*How do you cope with all this hair* she coos
Polite exasperation failing to mask the frustration
she would evidently be sharing later
by the shabby chic coffee machine.

I look up at her sharply
through a jungle of soggy creepers.

Blood over grit
Time over blood
Grit over time.

THE END

# INAPPROPRIATE ENCORE

# ROALD DAHL REAL DOLL

I want a Roald Dahl real doll:
A plastic
fantastic
Mr fox
in a box
with a kink for gingham
and knee high socks.

Looking relaxed and nicely overfed,
reclining in the armchair by my bed,
with a screw on head.

A Dirty Beast.
A BFG,
who blows bubbles of erotic fantasy
with genitals as big as his ears
and enough metaphorical skill
to bring me to tears.

A pose-able,
bendable,
penis extendable,
totally dependable,
uniquely fashioned fabler.
A creativity enabler
with a passion for peaches
and bottle green breeches,
and a stonka of a Willy Wonka
I can smear in liquid chocolate.

I want a legendary narrator
in the guise of a six-foot masturbator
with sculpted latex wrinkles
and that special Roald Dahl twinkle,
able to tinkle out his winkle
the most Marvellous of Medicine.

I want a Roald Dahl real doll
with a mighty minstrel's soul
and an anatomically correct rectal hole.
I want a 7-inch deep oral cavity
dribbling the finest bardic vocabulary
I want revolting rhymes,
Tales of the unexpected,
I want his genius resurrected.

I want to prop him up under a tree
and let him tell great tales to me
while I sip from a flask of Tetley tea.
I want to hear his words and let them linger
as I get touched-up by the Magic Finger.

I want to be spread like pages,
excited in carefully constructed plotted stages.
I want my preconceptions
ripped from their gilded cages
with optional adventures
for a range of ages.
I want him to tickle
the whole spectrum of sensation
as he opens, not my legs
but my imagination.

I want a Roald Dahl real doll
but I don't want to find him online or by phone,
I want to browse for him
in one of thousands of council run
pimped out literature houses
where the librarians sterilise the products
wearing spongeable trousers
and unbuttoned blouses.

I want to explore the whole canon of authors
from Horny to Dickens,
Hardy to Lear,

I want to plunder their passion
stick my tongue in each ear.

But first I want to rent out
a Roald Dahl real doll,
a literary sex toy that I can call mine,
allowing my limbs and my brain cells
to fully entwine
around his life like design,
before returning him clean and intact
to avoid a library fine.

Then I promise my parents
I'll rent out someone
a little more adult.
Next time.

# THANKS & ACKNOWLEDGEMENTS

I'd like to thank adrenaline, honesty and courage for helping me write, shape and perform these poems in front of actual real people, many of whom were holding glass objects.

I'd also like to honour my husband Rich, for truly being okay with me writing about his face and the softest, wettest parts of our relationship, despite the fact he's so painfully introverted, it's hard to get him to open the curtains.

To all those people who have read, advised, edited and supported my writing over the years, particularly in this collection, with special thanks to Morgan Rivers and David Oakwood for their early editing of these pages.

To Jonny Fluffypunk and Chris Redmond for sharing the Hip Yak Poetry Shack adventure with me and to all the shining honest funny clever poets out there, you make me happy all the time. This goes double for Matt Harvey and Beryl the Feral, two of the most wonder-filled and wonderful poets and people I know.

Finally, I want to thank my daughter Matilda and my son Wilfred, who have inspired so many of the poems in *Show Me Life* and who, despite their best finger poking efforts, have not yet managed to delete all the lovely, embarassing and desperate things I have written about them. Things, which on reflection, make this not so much a poetry book but an elaborate cry for help.

I love you.

To the moon and back again.

Now put your shoes on.

Printed in January 2023
by Rotomail Italia S.p.A., Vignate (MI) - Italy